Kenai Fjords, *Alaska's Jewel in the Rough,* was published by Denali Images. Book concepts, design and photography by Steve Gilroy with text written by Jim Pfeiffenberger.

ISBN # 1-882945-05-0

Printed by Northern Printing, Anchorage, Alaska.

Acknowledgement

As my career unfolds I am continually amazed at the grace I've been given and all of the opportunities I have been able to embrace. The completion of this, my first book, is one of them.

If there exists a single recipe for success, it is quite apparent that surrounding oneself with quality people and relying on their own special gifts is the first essential ingredient. This is certainly what brought this book project to fruition.

I am especially grateful to Tom Tongas of Kenai Fjords Tours for his generous support of this project, for the vision he has, and for the energy and enthusiasm he possesses. I would also like to thank the Alaska Natural History Association at Kenai Fjords for their support and for their encouragement.

When choosing a writer for this book, the decision actually required little thought. After speaking with Jim Pfeiffenberger for a short time, it became quickly apparent that Kenai Fjords is more than just a pretty place. It is a personal refuge and a place he calls home whether at work or at play. Without his intimate knowledge of Kenai Fjords or his sensitivity to the area, my images would have had no story to tell.

And last, but certainly not least, I want to thank Connie Engelbrecht for lending me the use of her lovely artwork. Although her designs add a wonderful complement to the layout of this book, I assure you they look even better on the tiles, trivets, coffee mugs & oak boxes they normally appear upon!

Kenai Fjords National Park

Alaska's Jewel in the Rough

 Geology

 Marine Life

 Bird Life

 Sightseeing & Recreation

Written by Jim Pfeiffenberger

Kenai Fjords National Park

Geology

"I'm standing on a smooth granite knob high above the sea. Towering overhead, rock walls partially veiled by fractured curtains of ice rise over four thousand feet. Below, the water is filled with glowing blue icebergs that crackle as they gently shift and roll. I watch closely, waiting for the lapping tide to rip loose another berg.

A series of loud pops echoes off the fjord walls and what appears to be a shower of dusty ice particles begins to rain down from the glacier's face. The splashes they make reveal that these are not mere dust-sized particles, but rather, huge slabs of ice the size of automobiles and refrigerators.

As the shower of falling debris shatters the ocean surface, a low rumbling sound reverberates. Soon the entire face of the glacier shifts into pseudo-slow-motion and the rumbling transforms into a thundering roar. In just a few seconds, massive sheets of ice that took hundreds of years to form collapse in a single cataclysmic finale. Powerless and numb, I suddenly feel a panic-stricken urge to retreat to my kayak but by then it is all over. Now only a huge wave rolling across the fjord testifies to the grand performance. I sit for a while longer awed by the powerful forces surrounding me."

A contrast of shapes and colors creates a stunning beauty in Three Hole Bay.

There is nothing subtle about the beauty of Kenai Fjords National Park. It is evident with every new view encountered behind each rocky headland, along every knife-edged ridge, and with every ominous rumble from a calving blue glacier. It is a spectacular beauty, at once stunning and completely over-whelming. It is a rugged beauty resulting from geological forces that have no regard for human time or scale. It is a beauty that remains as wild and unre-strained as it has been throughout the millennia.

The forces which create the Kenai Fjords are colossal. In fact, Kenai Fjords National Park sits at the edge of a geological danger zone where colli-sions between the North American continental plate and the Pacific Oceanic plate cause frequent, sometimes catastrophic earthquakes. As these plates grind together, the Pacific plate is forced downward, dragging the edge of the North American plate with it. This results in a sinking, or subsiding, coast-line. In reality, the Kenai Mountains are slowly drowning in the ocean.

A long term result of this process is that glacial features once found in upper alpine zones now lie at water's edge. For instance, the gracefully curv-ing bays and coves of the Aialik and Harris peninsulas are glacial cirques that were once well above tidewater. More recent signs of this subsiding coastline

Lush vegetation and cascading waterfalls continue to shape the landscape in Aialik Bay.

can be observed along the beaches lined with silvery "ghost forests." These trees were killed when the 1964 quake dropped the shoreline up to six feet, drowning the roots in salt water.

The most obvious forces shaping Kenai Fjords are the glaciers which carve and grind away at the mountains as they flow downhill. Giants like Aialik, Holgate, Northwestern and McCarty patiently move tons of rock, deepening and steepening the fjord walls. As immense as each of these glaciers appears to those visiting Kenai Fjords for the first time, it is even harder to comprehend the vast source of their origin.

The Kenai Mountains are home to one of the largest subarctic icefield and glacier systems in the world. Storms sweeping in from the Gulf of Alaska dump hundreds and perhaps thousands of inches of snow on the Kenai Mountains each winter. Since the summers are too cool and too short to melt it all, there is a perpetual surplus of snow. It collects high in the mountains in a vast oval basin more than thirty miles long and twenty miles wide. There it lies buried, compressed, and eventually transformed into glacier ice.

This frozen wilderness, known as the Harding Icefield, has existed for tens of thousands of years. It is a remnant of the last ice age and it is also the

The stunning beauty of Northwestern Fjord is characterized by raw earth that was exposed when glaciers retreated from this area during the 1900's.

A massive sheet of ice topples from the face of the Holgate Glacier during a procession of spectacular performances.

Many plant species colonize the rock fissures along Kenai Fjords' cliff edges revealing the early phases of vegetation.

largest icefield in the United States. Like a high alpine lake which empties into streams and rivers, the Harding Icefield feeds more than thirty-five glaciers which flow outward in all directions. To the west, they flow gently down to broad, open flatlands where they empty into a myriad of lakes and rivers. To the east, however, they drop steeply to the sea, where they crack and rumble as they release icebergs into Kenai Fjords.

Throughout the centuries, these tidewater glaciers have repeatedly advanced and retreated, like icy tentacles reaching out and retracting again and again. In Holgate Arm, the most recent retreat took place in the 1600's. Since that time, vegetation has invaded the fjord walls and today they are well covered with spruce forests and brushy alder patches. In Northwestern and McCarty Fjords, the retreat of the glaciers took place during the 1900's. Here, freshly scoured bedrock and piles of debris bulldozed by glaciers dominate the scene. This fresh, raw land is being slowly claimed by the coastal forest until it is all scraped clean again by the glaciers of some future century.

The grinding glaciers, the shifting tides, the devastating earthquakes all proceed to shape and change Kenai Fjords on their own patient schedules. We can only glimpse what amounts to a tiny moment in this grand scheme, and even that can stagger the senses.

The majestic mountains of Aialik Bay are seen through a key-hole shaped opening in Three Hole Bay.

In the years following a glacial retreat, low vegetation may eventually grow into lush coastal rainforests such as this one along the outer fringes of Northwestern Fjord.

*Soft hues of pink and orange
are seen during a sunset
over the vast expanse of the
Harding Icefield.*

Photo by Jim Pfeiffenberger

Kenai Fjords National Park

Marine Life

Nature's Rich Bounty

"I'm watching a harbor seal resting quietly on a drifting iceberg. Laying on its side with eyes half closed, it dozes serenely with an almost happy look on its face.

The ice bobs gently up and down with the rhythm of the sea and it lulls me into a light sleep. Suddenly I hear the distinct sound of a blow hole cracking the silence. The seal hears it, too. Its head snaps up instantly and its lazy look is immediately transformed into one of alertness. Together, our eyes search amongst the sparkling blue bergs and we listen intently. This time we hear a second, then a third, sharp, breathy blast.

The seal shifts from its side to its belly, clearly apprehensive now. I dip my paddle and stroke once to turn in the direction the seal is looking. This time I see them. One tall dorsal fin and two shorter ones cutting the water. Black backs glistening, each orca releases a misty breath, inhales deeply and slips beneath the surface.

The seal now looks panic-stricken and flops nervously looking from side to side. When the whales surface again, however, they are further away from us, seemingly unaware of both the plump seal and of me in my kayak. They surface again, and again, moving toward the upper fjord. I continue to watch intently until I can no longer hear or see them. The seal watches, too.

With the whales out of sight the seal shifts its body and hops awk-wardly toward the center of the berg. It then takes one last, long look in the direction of the whales. Satisfied, it rolls onto its side, arches its back, and dozes off with the same almost happy look on its face. I paddle away quietly, hoping my departure won't disturb its watchful rest."

Sea otters often lie on their backs while feeding and they are able to propel themselves along by paddling with their hind feet.

If the geological forces are what make Kenai Fjords stunning, the marine mammals are what make them exhilarating. The sight of a humpback whale gracefully arching its back and tail, or a sea otter bobbing gently with a pup on its belly, will often leave a deeper impression on visitors than the scenic grandeur of the glaciers and peaks.

The smallest of all marine mammals, the sea otter is just one of many creatures that calls the Kenai Fjords home. They typically weigh less than 100 pounds and have neither the bulk nor blubber that most marine mammals rely upon to insulate themselves from the cold. To compensate for this difference, sea otters are covered by the densest and most luxurious fur of any animal known. In fact, an adult sea otter will have up to 650,000 individual hair fibers in just one square inch of pelt. When this rich fur was discovered by early Russian and European explorers it commanded such a high price that the sea otter was nearly hunted into extinction .

Today, under protection of international treaty, sea otters are once again abundant along much of Alaska's coast. They live year-round in the fjords where they feed on shellfish in the rich intertidal zone. They usually forage in water less than 100 feet deep, diving to collect their prey and then returning

*Humpback whales often
raise their tales gracefully
into the air immediately
before the start of a deep
dive.*

The front flippers of a Steller sea lion not only facilitate its ability to swim in the water, but also to walk around on rookery ledges. In this photo it used them to propel itself into the air for an impressive dive.

to the surface to eat. Sometimes they lay a small rock on their chest and smash shellfish open to get at the soft insides.

Another year-round resident in the Kenai Fjords is the harbor seal. In the early summer months, the females gather and haul-out on floating ice near tidewater glaciers. It is here, in relative safety from predators, that they bear their young. Even the most thunderous glacier calvings hardly elicit a response from the resting mothers and their nursing pups. Other times of the year, lone seals may be seen swimming the nearshore waters in search of fish. They are easy to tell from sea otters by their big, deep-set eyes. They are also more than twice as large and much more rotund.

An even larger marine mammal patrolling the fjord waters is the Steller sea lion. They often travel in groups, sometimes playfully "porpoising" and splashing as they swim. Their dark tan color as well as their size sets them apart from the seals and otters. Females average 7 feet long and weigh 600 lbs, while the males grow up to 9 feet long and reach over 1500 lbs in weight. They haul out in large numbers in the Chiswell Islands where granite shelves are worn smooth from generations of sea lion flesh. Here you'll see another distinct sea lion characteristic – their agility on land. Unlike harbor seals, they can pull their hind flippers up under their bodies, stand up on their front flippers, and "walk" rather than simply flopping. Watching these hulking beasts belch and bellow as they jockey for the best sunning spot is an unforgettable part of a visit to the fjords.

Equally unforgettable are the whales and porpoises that inhabit Kenai Fjords. Graceful giants like the humpback whale migrate thousands of miles each summer from their winter calving grounds to feed in the fjords. Alaska's long hours of daylight combine with the cold, nutrient rich waters to create an abundance of plankton, small fish, and other creatures. The fjord waters become a rich, living broth that the humpbacks consume in enormous quantities. Cow-calf pairs are often seen lingering for weeks at a time in the same location, sustaining themselves on this bounty. The calves may eventually reach 35 tons and live for half a century.

Visitors to Kenai Fjords are sometimes treated to playful displays when Dall's porpoises approach the bow of a sightseeing boat.

Photo by Patrick Endres

Orcas also frequent these rich feeding grounds. They are toothed whales that feed on fish, squid, birds, and even other marine mammals like seals and porpoises. Highly social, orcas travel in pods of 3 to 40 animals. They navigate and find prey by echolocation, emitting clicks as they swim. They also communicate to each other with strange underwater squeals, squeaks, and groans – mysterious conversations that we only recently became aware of. The tall, black dorsal fins of the males, up to six feet high, are unmistakable.

Their smaller cousin, the Dall's porpoise, is possibly the most exciting marine mammal to encounter in the fjord waters. They are swift, spirited swimmers with a habit of appearing out of nowhere and "bow-riding" on the pressure wave in front of a boat. Watching them dart through the water, break the surface at high speed, and shoot a blast of sea spray into the air is one of the fjords finer thrills.

Orcas roam throughout much of coastal Alaska and spend much of their time following large schools of migrating salmon. This pod, seen with Bear Glacier in the distance, was photographed during a silver salmon migration which usually occurs each fall.

A young humpback whale thrusts out of the water in a behavior known as "breaching." The reasons whales leap from the water's surface is not completely understood.

This sea otter was caught napping as it bobbed along with the flow of the tide.

A group of Steller sea lions snooze together along the edge of a favorite sunning ledge in the Chiswell Islands.

A humpback whale smashes the surface with a sweeping motion of its fluke, or tail. Distinctive markings on each humpback fluke allow researchers to identify individual whales.

Kenai Fjords National Park

Bird Life

Bird Life in the Fjords

"I am staring at a crowded ledge lined with hundreds of common murres. Around them, the cliffs are alive with thousands of chattering kittiwakes, and below the waters are busy with feeding puffins. A lone bald eagle appears above the cliff, and the chattering immediately turns into a communal scream as the kittiwakes take to the air. The puffins begin to dive and disappear beneath the ocean surface, seeking refuge from the looming predator. As the eagle glides effortlessly past the colony, kittiwakes swirl in its wake. Suddenly, the eagle takes an evasive dive. I raise my binoculars and spy a peregrine falcon swooping down at the eagle. After several aggressive attacks by the falcon, the eagle finally changes direction. It will have to find prey elsewhere. The peregrine resumes its perch atop a nearby snag. One by one, the puffins pop back to the ocean surface. The uproar slowly subsides to a busy chatter as the kittiwakes settle back onto their nests, and the rhythm of the colony continues beneath the watchful falcon's eye."

A pair of horned puffins keep a watchful eye for predators atop this fairly exposed perch.

Birds, with their restless energy and perpetual activity, bring a sense of vitality to Kenai Fjords. While the marine mammals can be elusive at times, the birds are everywhere. They are extroverts whose mating displays take place in plain, public view. Their squabbles are always apparent, their opinions always voiced. They form frenetic societies at the edge of the open sea, where many species are crammed together in high-rise housing complexes. The short duration of summer only intensifies their sense of urgency–build nest, find food, raise young before summer's daylight wanes and winter storms return.

Puffins, murres, murrelets, and auklets belong to a family of birds known as Alcids. Strong diving birds and weak flyers, Alcids are sometimes called the "penguins of the north." Though not truly flightless like penguins, they have stubby wings, and some puffins are even known to get so overstuffed with fish that they cannot get airborne, no matter how much they flap. With ten different species of Alcids present, including many not easily viewed elsewhere, the fjords are a birdwatcher's paradise.

Puffins draw the most attention for first-time visitors to the fjords. With their big red and yellow bills, bright orange feet, black wing feathers, and

Common murres often occupy cliff edges in crammed fashion. This seemingly overcrowded style helps them protect their eggs from possible intruders.

A stunning yellow feather sweeping gracefully behind the eye easily distinguishes the tufted puffin from its cousin, the horned puffin.

clean white breasts, horned puffins resemble clowns in formal dinner wear. It takes several years to develop this full adult garb. A close look reveals the tiny "horn" of fleshy tissue above their eyes that gives them their name.

Horned puffins nest by the thousands in the Chiswell Islands, a part of the the Alaska Maritime National Wildlife Refuge that is just offshore from Kenai Fjords National Park. The steep granite walls and distance from shore provide excellent protection from predators, and the fish-filled waters provide ample food. They nest in naturally occurring cracks and crevices in the rock walls and lay just one egg each breeding season. They pursue fish by "flying" underwater with swift, strong wingbeats. Fine serrations on the inside of their bills allow them to hold and carry a dozen or more of their slippery prey at one time. Throughout late June and all of July, horned puffins can be seen disappearing into dark crevices with loads of freshly caught fish for their chicks.

Tufted puffins also nest by the thousands in the Chiswell Islands. Their all black bodies and long, blond tufts of feathers flowing back from behind their eyes set them apart from their "horned" cousins. Like their close cousins, they also "fly" underwater in pursuit of small fish, have serrated bills, and take several years to develop the full plumage and bill associated with adulthood. Unlike their cousins, they make their nests by digging deep burrows into the soil that tops the Chiswell Islands. Both species spend the entire winter on the open sea and return to land only for the short summer breeding season. Individual tufted puffins are known to return to the same burrow year after year.

Another conspicuous Alcid in the Chiswell Islands is the common murre. Common murres truly look dressed for a formal affair with their black head, wings and back, and their pure white breast. In March, they gather on the ocean surface in dense rafts of thousands of birds as they prepare for breeding. They do not seek a crack or burrow, but instead nest upon open, narrow rock ledges, building no nest whatsoever. The apparent risk of this nesting style is offset by the shape of the murre's egg. It is wide and round at one end, and tapers rapidly to a narrow, almost pointed tip at the

A group of common murres line a cliff edge while keeping a watchful eye out for predators.

other end. The result of this cone shape is that if the egg is bumped or disturbed, it pivots around the narrow end and simply rolls in a tight circle, instead of rolling off the edge of the cliff. The birds afford further protection to their eggs by nesting side by side in dense colonies. Any predator attempting to swoop down and steal eggs or chicks is met by scores of sharp, upturned murre bills. These bills are designed not only for defense, but also for catching and holding a single fish lengthwise.

The difference in nesting styles and needs of these alcid species allows them to share the same cliffs and islands without directly competing for space. Other alcids found here include thick-billed murres, marbled murrelets, Kittlitz's murrelets, ancient murrelets, pigeon guillemots, rhinoceros auklets and parakeet auklets. As if that's not enough, the fjords and surrounding islands are used as breeding grounds by pelagic cormorants, red-faced cormorants, glaucous-winged gulls, black-legged kittiwakes, fork-tailed storm petrels, arctic terns, mew gulls, red-breasted mergansers, black oyster catchers, and semipalmated plovers among others.

Peregrine falcons are also regular nesters along the Kenai Fjords coastline. Just as seabirds are drawn here by the abundance of fish, the peregrines are drawn by the abundance of seabirds. Circling high above the water, they will suddenly plunge after their prey in a steep power dive at speeds

A red-faced cormorant is one bird of an eclectic array of species that come to nest in the Kenai Fjords.

A pair of mated bald eagles scan the water below, apparently looking for a fish close enough to the surface to warrant a possible attempt.

Parakeet auklets are one of several different members of the Alcid family that make their home in Kenai Fjords.

approaching 200 miles per hour. To them, the busy Chiswell Islands are not so much a high-rise apartment complex as they are a fast food joint. The falcons nourish their young on the plenty, and fatten themselves for the long journey south to their wintering grounds.

A more permanent coastal resident is the bald eagle. These magnificent birds can be seen soaring above the fjords almost any time of year. More than 100 of their huge, stick nests have been found along the Park's coast, usually up high in a Sitka spruce. They are territorial birds, preferring a commanding view of their surroundings. Adult pairs fend off intruding eagles during the summer, and may hatch and raise up to three eaglets at a time, feeding them primarily with fish. During the winter months, they become more tolerant of one another and congregate along open estuaries where food is more plentiful. With their regal looks and six foot wing spans they are well suited to the spectacular surroundings. If these majestic fjords were palaces, the eagles would surely be kings.

*A bald eagle lifts itself
from the ocean surface
following a successful
snatch of a small herring.*

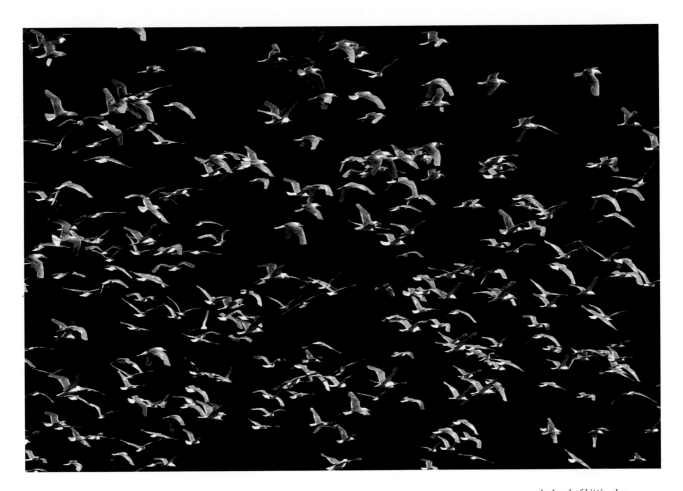

A cloud of kittiwakes take flight in a panic-stricken flurry initiated by a swooping Peregrine falcon.

Kenai Fjords National Park

Sightseeing & Recreation

Exploring Kenai Fjords

"There is one word of advice and caution to be given those intending to visit Alaska for pleasure, for sightseeing. If you are old, go by all means; but if you are young, wait. The scenery of Alaska is much grander than anything else of the kind in the world, and it is not well to dull one's capacity for enjoyment by seeing the finest first."

Henry Gannet, chief geographer, The Harriman Expedition, 1899

Four ocean kayakers pause while taking in this awesome view of a tidewater glacier.

To both visitors and Alaskan residents, Kenai Fjords National Park may indeed be one of the most stunning places on earth. It contains an abundance of everything that is spectacular about Alaska's coastline – thundering tidewater glaciers, storm-blasted sea stacks, breaching humpback whales, seabirds by the thousands, salmon-choked streams, and jagged, snow-covered peaks. For those lucky enough to see the fjords on a beautiful summer day, Henry Gannett's words certainly ring true – all else may pale by comparison.

Most visitors to Kenai Fjords experience its beauty from the comfort of a private tour boat. A small fleet of vessels ply the fjord waters during the summer months, making these some of the most accessible tidewater glaciers and seabird rookeries in all of Alaska, and in the world. A typical day trip might include watching huge icebergs falling from the face of a glacier, seeing sea otters bobbing on their backs, sea lions jostling for position on a rookery ledge, orcas rising and spouting, puffins buzzing to and fro, and bald eagles perched high on their nests. It's no wonder more and more people come to experience the Kenai Fjords each year.

A tour boat sits in front of the Holgate Glacier hoping to see ice calve from its steep-sided face.

A myriad of beautiful wildflowers may be seen along any of the hiking trails near the Exit Glacier.

Photo by Jim Pfeiffenberger

Fireweed is one of the first flowering plant species to invade newly exposed soil.

More adventurous visitors may choose to explore the Kenai Fjords by kayak. This is how the original inhabitants of this rugged coastline traveled for generations, following the seasonal movements of sea mammals and fish. By the late 1800's, contact with European explorers had so decimated these local populations that no villages remained. Today, with the advent of modern kayaks, the waters are once again stirred by the stroke of the paddle. For many, ocean kayaking provides a powerful and intimate experience in this coastal wilderness.

Kenai Fjords National Park also boasts one of the most accessible land-borne glaciers in Alaska. Like the tidewater glaciers of the park's coastline, Exit Glacier flows down from the vast Harding Icefield. A short walk on a flat, easy trail leads to the edge of this impressive spectacle which often glows brilliantly with surreal shades of blue. Perhaps most impressive of all is its towering walls, cracked and crevassed into fantastic ice sculptures which rise steeply overhead.

The bare, rock-strewn ground and scraped valley walls tell of the glacier's once even greater magnitude. The surrounding vegetation also tells a story of forest formation. From the spruce stands at the park's boundary to the cottonwoods in the parking lot, or the patchy flowers,

A gentle hike along a designated park service trail allows many people to enjoy an up-close look at Exit Glacier.

moss, and alders near the front of the glacier, the various stages of vegetation patiently colonize this newly exposed earth.

From Exit Glacier, a steep trail leads up the mountainside toward the Harding Icefield. The trail rises quickly and affords dramatic views of Exit Glacier and the sprawling valley beyond. In July and early August, this high country is sprinkled with colors from wildflowers like pink fireweed, glowing purple Nootka lupine, yellow snapdragons, chocolate lilies, and lovely wild geraniums. These high meadows are also frequented by mountain goats and black bears seeking succulent young shoots to feed upon. At the end of the trail, hikers are rewarded with one of the finest views in southcentral Alaska. Below, Exit Glacier flows in fissured patterns of twisted blue ice. Behind, the Resurrection River meanders through a broad, glacial swath through the Kenai Mountains. Ahead, the vast, frozen expanse of the Harding Icefield extends to the horizon, interrupted only by occasional "nunataks," an Eskimo word for the "lonely peaks" that jut out of the icefield. The ice age still reins supreme in this pocket of the earth.

For experienced mountaineers, the Harding Icefield offers an inviting challenge. Like islands in a calm, cool sea, the shores of the

An aerial flightseeing tour of the Kenai Fjords provides a completely different and often overwhelming perspective of its grandeur and beauty.

Photo by Susan Pfeiffenberger.

distant nunataks beckon and beg to be explored. Such adventure has its risks, though. Crevasses lurk beneath the surface, and storms can strike suddenly and ferociously. In excess of 700 square miles, this is the largest icefield in the United States, and to this day, relatively few have penetrated its inner reaches.

More commonly, people experience the Harding Icefield from the air. An aerial flightseeing tour provides a dramatic and exhilarating perspective that will likely never be forgotten. Waves of windblown snow sweep across the frozen plain like desert sands. The fjords line up in crooked rows, like skinny ocean fingers grasping at the mountains. Ridge after ridge of jagged peaks recede into the distance until the shining Gulf of Alaska swallows them all. You can practically take in the entire park in one long, high, splendid view. Seen from this angle, the fjords, though hardly diminished, can look small. As the edge of the far horizon curves away, it is clear that Kenai Fjords National Park is just one corner of this globe, one finite wilderness set aside for its beauty, one rare jewel in the rough where life carries on amidst the rhythm of the tides and the patient pulse of the glaciers.

A more obscure beauty of the Kenai Fjords lies in the intertidal zones where a myriad of starfish and sea urchins are among many organisms and crustaceans living here.

About the Photographer

Steve Gilroy spends much of his time roaming wild and remote parts of Alaska. He leads custom photography tours throughout Alaska and resides in Talkeetna. In addition to his travels in Alaska, his passion for outdoor photography has taken him on repeated trips to Africa, Russia and Central & South America. His work has been featured in *Outdoor Photographer, Outside, Sierra, Discover, The Geographical, Alaska Airlines Magazine, United Airlines, Patagonia Inc., AT&T* and other magazines, book publications and company brochures.